Martin Luther King Jr.

MARTIN LUTHER KING, JR.
(1929–1968)

Quotations

OF

*Martin
Luther
King,
Jr.*

APPLEWOOD BOOKS
Carlisle, Massachusetts

Copyright ©2004 Applewood Books, Inc.

Thank you for purchasing an Applewood Book. Applewood reprints America's lively classics — books from the past that are still of interest to modern readers. For a free copy of our current catalog, please write to Applewood Books, P.O. Box 27, Carlisle, MA 01741.

www.awb.com

ISBN 978-1-4290-9380-4

10 9 8 7 6 5 4 3 2

Manufactured in the U.S.A.

Martin Luther King, Jr.

MARTIN LUTHER KING, JR. was born on January 15, 1929 in Atlanta, Georgia. He was the second child of Reverend Martin Luther King, Sr. and Alberta Williams King.

In 1934, he started school before reaching the legal age of six. When it was discovered, he was asked to leave until the following year. He excelled in school, skipping both ninth and twelfth grades. At the age of fifteen, Martin entered Morehouse College.

Martin Luther King, Jr. was ordained in 1948. Reverend King became Assistant Pastor of Ebenezer Baptist Church. Also that year, he graduated Morehouse College with a B.A. degree in Sociology. After graduating, he attended the Crozer Theological Seminary in Chester, Pennsylvania, simultaneously attending the University of Pennsylvania. In 1951, he received a Bachelor of Divinity degree from Crozer.

Reverend King moved to Boston in 1951 to begin a doctoral program at Boston University. In 1953, he married Coretta Scott. Together, they had four children: Yolanda Denise, Martin Luther III, Dexter Scott, and Bernice Albertine. In 1954, Reverend King became the pastor of Dexter Avenue Baptist Church in Montgomery, Alabama.

In 1955, he received a Ph.D. in Systematic Theology from Boston University.

In 1959, Dr. King resigned from Dexter Avenue Baptist Church to move to Atlanta to direct his recently-founded Southern Christian Leadership Conference. In Atlanta, he also served as co-pastor with his father at Ebenezer Baptist Church.

Dr. King was a central figure in the Civil Rights Movement and a leading advocate of non-violence. In 1963, at the age of 34, he was named "Man of the Year" by Time Magazine. In 1964, he was awarded the Nobel Peace Prize, the youngest man and the first black man to receive that honor. Over the years, he was arrested thirty times for his civil rights actions. Dr. King was a member of a number of national and Atlanta-based boards of directors, in profit and non-profit organizations. Dr. King was elected to the American Academy of Arts and Sciences and other learned societies.

On April 4, 1968, Dr. King was in Memphis to help lead sanitation workers in a protest. As he stood on the balcony of the Lorraine Motel, he was shot and killed by James Earl Ray.

QUOTATIONS
OF
*Martin
Luther
King,
Jr.*

Quotations of Martin Luther King, Jr.

Now, I say to you today my friends, even though we face the difficulties of today and tomorrow, I still have a dream. It is a dream deeply rooted in the American dream. I have a dream that one day this nation will rise up and live out the true meaning of its creed:—"We hold these truths to be self-evident, that all men are created equal."

I have a dream that my four little children will one day live in a nation where they will not be judged by the color of their skin, but by the content of their character.

I have a dream that one day every valley shall be exalted, every hill and mountain shall be made low, the rough places will be made straight and the glory of the Lord shall be revealed and all flesh shall see it together.

Quotations of Martin Luther King, Jr.

I have a dream that one day on the red hills of Georgia, the sons of former slaves and the sons of former slave owners will be able to sit together at the table of brotherhood.

*A*ll men are caught in an inescapable network of mutuality.

*O*ur loyalties must transcend our race, our tribe, our class, and our nation; and this means we must develop a world perspective.

Quotations of Martin Luther King, Jr.

I want to be the white man's brother, not his brother-in-law.

*T*here can be no deep disappointment where there is not deep love.

*I*n the end, we will remember not the words of our enemies, but the silence of our friends.

Quotations of Martin Luther King, Jr.

*L*ife's most persistent and urgent question is, "What are you doing for others?".

*T*he hope of a secure and livable world lies with disciplined nonconformists who are dedicated to justice, peace and brotherhood.

*T*he good neighbor looks beyond the external accidents and discerns those inner qualities that make all men human and, therefore, brothers.

Quotations of Martin Luther King, Jr.

All labor that uplifts humanity has dignity and importance and should be undertaken with painstaking excellence.

If a man is called to be a streetsweeper, he should sweep streets even as Michelangelo painted, or Beethoven composed music, or Shakespeare wrote poetry. He should sweep streets so well that all the hosts of heaven and earth will pause to say, here lived a great streetsweeper who did his job well.

Almost always, the creative dedicated minority has made the world better.

Quotations of Martin Luther King, Jr.

Every man must decide whether he will walk in the light of creative altruism or in the darkness of destructive selfishness.

We are not makers of history. We are made by history.

Philanthropy is commendable, but it must not cause the philanthropist to overlook the circumstances of economic injustice which make philanthropy necessary.

Quotations of Martin Luther King, Jr.

I submit that an individual who breaks a law that conscience tells him is unjust, and who willingly accepts the penalty of imprisonment in order to arouse the conscience of the community over its injustice, is in reality expressing the highest respect for the law.

*I*t may be true that the law cannot make a man love me, but it can stop him from lynching me, and I think that's pretty important.

*I*njustice anywhere is a threat to justice everywhere.

Quotations of Martin Luther King, Jr.

The moral arc of the universe bends at the elbow of justice.

Law and order exist for the purpose of establishing justice and when they fail in this purpose they become the dangerously structured dams that block the flow of social progress.

Never forget that everything Hitler did in Germany was legal.

Quotations of Martin Luther King, Jr.

I have decided to stick with love. Hate is too great a burden to bear.

*L*ove is the only force capable of transforming an enemy into friend.

*H*atred paralyzes life; love releases it.
Hatred confuses life; love harmonizes it.
Hatred darkens life; love illuminates it.

Like an unchecked cancer, hate corrodes the personality and eats away its vital unity. Hate destroys a man's sense of values and his objectivity. It causes him to describe the beautiful as ugly and the ugly as beautiful, and to confuse the true with the false and the false with the true.

Never succumb to the temptation of bitterness.

Take the first step in faith. You don't have to see the whole staircase, just take the first step.

Man was born into barbarism when killing his fellow man was a normal condition of existence. He became endowed with a conscience. And he has now reached the day when violence toward another human being must become as abhorrent as eating another's flesh.

Everything that we see is a shadow cast by that which we do not see.

Darkness cannot drive out darkness; only light can do that. Hate cannot drive out hate; only love can do that.

Quotations of Martin Luther King, Jr.

Have we not come to such an impasse in the modern world that we must love our enemies—or else? The chain reaction of evil—hate begetting hate, wars producing more wars—must be broken, or else we shall be plunged into the dark abyss of annihilation.

I decided early to give my life to something eternal and absolute. Not to these little gods that are here today and gone tomorrow, but to God who is the same yesterday, today, and forever.

Our lives begin to end the day we become silent about things that matter.

*E*ven if I knew that tomorrow the world would go to pieces, I would still plant my apple tree.

*I*f physical death is the price that I must pay to free my white brothers and sisters from a permanent death of the spirit, then nothing can be more redemptive.

*E*verybody can be great. . . because anybody can serve. You don't have to have a college degree to serve. You don't have to make your subject and verb agree to serve. You only need a heart full of grace. A soul generated by love.

Quotations of Martin Luther King, Jr.

The time is always right to do what is right.

I submit to you that if a man hasn't discovered something he will die for, he isn't fit to live.

If we are to go forward, we must go back and rediscover those precious values—that all reality hinges on moral foundations and that all reality has spiritual control.

Quotations of Martin Luther King, Jr.

A lie cannot live.

I believe that unarmed truth and unconditional love will have the final word in reality. That is why right, temporarily defeated, is stronger than evil triumphant.

*W*e may have all come on differentships, but we're in the same boat now.

Quotations of Martin Luther King, Jr.

A nation or civilization that continues to produce soft-minded men purchases its own spiritual death on the installment plan.

The question is not whether we will be extremist but what kind of extremist will we be.

I look to a day when people will not be judged by the color of their skin, but by the content of their character.

Freedom is never voluntarily given by the oppressor; it must be demanded by the oppressed.

The ultimate measure of a man is not where he stands in moments of comfort and convenience, but where he stands at times of challenge and controversy.

Change does not roll in on the wheels of inevitability, but comes through continuous struggle. And so we must straighten our backs and work for our freedom. A man can't ride you unless your back is bent.

Before the Pilgrims landed at Plymouth, we were here. Before the pen of Jefferson etched across the pages of history the majestic words of the Declaration of Independence, we were here. If the inexpressible cruelties of slavery could not stop us, the opposition we now face will surely fail.

A right delayed is a right denied.

Segregation is the adultery of an illicit intercourse between injustice and immorality.

A riot is the language of the unheard.

Discrimination is a hellhound that gnaws at Negroes in every waking moment of their lives to remind them that the lie of their inferiority is accepted as truth in the society dominating them.

The sweltering summer of the Negro's legitimate discontent will not pass until there is an invigorating autumn of freedom and equality.

Quotations of Martin Luther King, Jr.

I refuse to accept the view that mankind is so tragically bound to the starless midnight of racism and war that the bright daybreak of peace and brotherhood can never become a reality.

*P*eace is not merely a distant goal that we seek, but a means by which we arrive at that goal.

*I*f you will protest courageously, and yet with dignity and Christian love, when the history books are written in future generations, the historians will have to pause and say, "There lived a great people—a black people—who injected new meaning and dignity into the veins of civilization."

We must build dikes of courage to hold back the flood of fear.

The limitation of riots, moral questions aside, is that they cannot win and their participants know it. Hence, rioting is not revolutionary but reactionary because it invites defeat. It involves an emotional catharsis, but it must be followed by a sense of futility.

If you succumb to the temptation of using violence in the struggle, unborn generations will be the recipients of a long and desolate night of bitterness, and your chief legacy to the future will be an endless reign of meaningless chaos.

We will have to repent in this generation not merely for the hateful words and actions of the bad people but for the appalling silence of the good people.

Nonviolence means avoiding not only external physical violence but also internal violence of spirit. You not only refuse to shoot a man, but you refuse to hate him.

Nonviolence is a powerful and just weapon which cuts without wounding and ennobles the man who wields it. It is a sword that heals.

Quotations of Martin Luther King, Jr.

Human salvation lies in the hands of the creatively maladjusted.

Nonviolence is the answer to the crucial political and moral questions of our time; the need for mankind to overcome oppression and violence without resorting to oppression and violence. Mankind must evolve for all human conflict a method which rejects revenge, aggression, and retaliation. The foundation of such a method is love.

Ten thousand fools proclaim themselves into obscurity, while one wise man forgets himself into immortality.

Quotations of Martin Luther King, Jr.

When you are right you cannot be too radical; when you are wrong, you cannot be too conservative.

All progress is precarious, and the solution of one problem brings us face to face with another problem.

Nothing in all the world is more dangerous than sincere ignorance and conscientious stupidity.

Quotations of Martin Luther King, Jr.

We must learn to live together as brothers or perish together as fools.

Our scientific power has outrun our spiritual power. We have guided missiles and misguided men.

Shallow understanding from people of good will is more frustrating than absolute misunderstanding from people of ill will.

Quotations of Martin Luther King, Jr.

One of the greatest casualties of the war in Vietnam is the Great Society . . . shot down on the battlefield of Vietnam.

I just want to do God's will. And he's allowed me to go to the mountain. And I've looked over, and I've seen the promised land. I may not get there with you, but I want you to know tonight that we as a people will get to the promised land. So I'm happy tonight. I'm not worried about anything. I'm not fearing any man.

Martin Luther King Jr.